Unless otherwise indicated, a
James Version, © 1979, 1980, 1982, 1984 by Thomas Nelson, Inc.

The Ten Greatest Prayers of the Bible

By Benjamin L. Reynolds, M.Min
Discover other titles at http://amazon.com/author/benjaminreynolds

For information, contact Benjamin L. Reynolds at
info@benjaminlreynolds.com or www.benjaminlreynolds.com

Ready for the Rapture
Seven Years Until Eternity: The Rise of the Antichrist
Living in the New Millennium and Beyond
40 Days of Faith

ISBN-13: 978-1463651497
ISBN-10: 146365149X

Printed in the United States of America
Copyright © 2010 by Benjamin L. Reynolds

Table of Contents

PREFACE

Often times when we read miraculous events of the Bible we think of them as only applying to the people who lived in biblical times. In our modern era of science, medicine and technology, people rarely rely on prayer to meet their needs. The purpose of writing this book is to show the importance of prayer and how it can be relative to people of all races, gender and social classes. Prayer is powerful and should be relied upon not only as a method of last resort, but in times when we don't think that we need it. Prayer is a useful tool for kings as well as common people. It was necessary for Christ, his Apostles, their congregations and is still necessary for us today.

I would like to give my personal testimonial about the power of prayer. A few years ago, the Lord delivered me from a sickness by the power of my prayer as well as the prayers of others. In September 2006, I had been suffering from Ulcerative Colitis and bleeding for several months. After spending several weeks in the hospital, I was cleared to go home for rest and recuperation. I was not showing much improvement at home and continued to bleed every time I went to the bathroom. Early one morning, I awoke and went into the bathroom where I continued to bleed severely as I had done for days. When I tried to walk back into the bedroom I passed out and fell on the floor. I don't know how long I was unconscious but my wife found me lying on the bathroom floor and she began trying to wake me. When I came to, I began gasping for air and was unable to breathe. Later we found out that this was due to having suffered severe blood loss and dehydration. My mother and aunt came upstairs after hearing my wife screaming and crying and called 911, and they helped my wife carry me back into the bedroom, where things only got worse. It was getting harder and harder to breathe. I felt my life slowly slipping away. After a few minutes, the struggle just became too great and I could barely keep my eyes open. At that moment I knew that I was going to die. As I lay on the floor there was a strange peace that came over me. I felt that I was living in my final moments. I looked up at my wife and whispered "I love you." I then closed my eyes and everything went black.

When I opened my eyes, I saw nothing but extreme darkness. It appeared that I was in a large open space, like a valley, with a black sky that had no stars. The ground beneath was blackish gray with cracks in it like a dry desert. Everything had the appearance of desolation. While there, the pain that had constantly been in my body for the past weeks had disappeared and I had intense feelings of fear and loneliness. I stood there for what appeared to be several minutes looking around and wondering what was happening. Having been a Christian for fourteen years and a pastor for the previous two years of my life, I was expecting to see something quite different in the afterlife. What I was seeing did not make any sense at all.

I thought to myself, *This cannot be all that there is in the afterlife! I have served God for too long and know that God is real. I*

4

have felt His love and Holy Spirit too many times. There must be a God and there must be a heaven! I began praying Psalm 23 and about halfway through, a bright flash appeared in the sky above me. When I looked up, I could see a large city with a bright gold aura, surrounded by angels in white robes. It was the city of New Jerusalem mentioned in Revelation 21 and 22.

Instantly, the loneliness seemed to vanish away as now I felt joy and relief from knowing that heaven was real and I would be going there. I then felt that there was something above and to my left. When I turned my head and looked, I saw more angels, who were closer and smiling. They were standing around someone who had a white robe with a golden belt, whose face shined with a white brightness so intense that I could not make out the features. I soon realized that this was Jesus Christ!

I tried to look into his face to make out His features, but the more that I stared, the brighter the light around his face became, forcing me to look away. Suddenly, I felt great shame and sorrow. I later realized what Daniel 10:8 meant when he said: "my comeliness in me is turned into corruption." Compared to the righteousness and holiness of God, I could feel the sin of my lowly human nature and knew that however righteous I may have thought that I was, it was nothing compared to God's true holiness. I felt so ashamed and embarrassed that I didn't want to look up at Jesus. I stared at the ground and thought, "*I wish that I could go to that city.*" Immediately a thunderous voice reverberated throughout my entire body and spirit saying to me; "You can come here if you want."

I looked up with excitement and thought that I wanted to go to the city above me. I was immediately propelled at and incredible speed up in the air towards the city just as quickly as I imagined going there. As I got closer, I could see that there were many angels surrounding the city and they were all smiling, with white robes and gold trumpets pressed to their lips. The city was completely made of gold, yet it had a white translucent glow that made it shine brightly. There were large walls with three gates on each made of white pearl.

It was very interesting to me that I saw large buildings, which resembled skyscrapers of different sizes behind the walls, which had what appeared to be windows. As I moved closer and closer at great speed, I felt that there was something behind me. I turned to look and a large screen suddenly appeared. I felt myself come to a stop. Different groups of people began to appear before me on the screen. Some I recognized as pastors and their wives, while others I did not know. At that point, a heavy burden for them and sadness swept over me. I quickly realized that it was God's burden for the ministry and mankind. I could not help but feel that the Lord showed me these people for a reason. At that moment, I understood that a decision had to be made. I thought, "Lord, they have no one to help them." Suddenly everything went dark and I felt myself back in my body again.

I momentarily retained the previous feeling of

euphoria and no pain. This was different after being so sick and full of pain for weeks. I could clearly notice the difference of not having any pain while I was outside of my body to then having the pain once again with the reuniting with my physical body.

I opened my eyes and saw my wife, mother and aunt above me crying. I also noticed that I was having trouble breathing again. As strange as it seems, this feeling was new, as I did not remember having the need to breathe before I returned. The paramedics arrived a little while later, put an oxygen mask on my face and took me to the hospital emergency room. I was given a blood transfusion and IV liquids through two PIC lines that were inserted directly into veins in my neck. The doctors told us that even in severe cases, it was normal to only use one PIC line into the vein to transfuse blood. However, because the situation was so critical, and I was in danger of imminently dying, they had no choice but to insert two lines. I had lost a great deal of blood and was severely dehydrated.

Later, after I had recovered, my wife told me that I was lifeless and not breathing when I was in her arms for at least five minutes back at the house. She had been rebuking the spirit of death and praying for God to put my life back in my body when I suddenly came back to life again.

This whole experience changed me. I knew that the Lord was dealing with me to give more of my life to him and to share my testimony of God's power with others. I began an intense study of all scriptures in the Bible that dealt with prayer, healing and the resurrection of the church. It is my belief that if we want to achieve the results that great people like Moses, David, Hezekiah and Solomon had, we must look at the prayers that they gave. These people were not just great because they did great things. A greater examination of scripture shows that they did great things because they prayed great prayers. I am fully convinced that if we enter into prayer and understand that prayer is a tool for achieving greatness, we will see the same miraculous wonders that our predecessors in the Bible saw. I know that I'm not alone in the belief that the only thing separating us from the great heroes of faith in the bible is the prayers we give. We have the same access and opportunity to reach out to God-but will we see the same results?

In writing the ten greatest prayers of the Bible, I used several criteria to select what I believed were truly the greatest prayers. I want to make it clear that in making my selections, it was not that the prayers I did not choose were not great; it was just that I personally felt that some were simply more outstanding. To begin, I made a list of what I felt were the greatest prayers in the Bible and then narrowed it down by looking at the overall impact of each prayer. To me, the most important aspect of the prayer people prayed was the results. Great prayers can, and should be, judged by their results. It's not like every prayer isn't important, I just believe that some prayers have a greater effect than others. I asked myself questions like: Who did the prayer impact? Did the prayer affect one person or a great number of people? Some prayers affected individuals, but a greater weight had to be given to prayers that affected more than one person.

Secondly, I looked at the person making the prayer. Was the person someone that anyone can relate to? This is important because I wanted to know if ordinary people could pray a similar prayer and achieve similar results if they found themselves in the same kind of situation as someone in the Bible. Thirdly, I looked at the circumstances the person was in. A person who encounters an average situation will pray an average prayer while a person undergoing extreme circumstances will pray extraordinary prayers.

As we look at the ten greatest prayers in the Bible, I hope that you will gain an appreciation for the power of prayer and come to realize that there is absolutely no difference between us and the people who prayed these great prayers. When we realize that we all have the same potential in prayer, then we will actualize it and see great results. I chose not to list the prayers in a 1 through 10 order of best to worst or worst to best because all were equally great and each showed unique characteristics about how to pray great prayers. The only prayer that I would say was the greatest, was the one prayed by Jesus Christ. Other than that, I give them all equal weight. I hope that in reading this book, you gain insight from those who prayed some of the greatest prayers, and that this book can in some way change you and those around you.

May God Bless you, and keep praying!

1

HANNAH'S PRAYER

The Prayer

"And she was in bitterness of soul, and prayed unto the LORD, and wept sore. And she vowed a vow, and said, O LORD of hosts, if thou wilt indeed look on the affliction of thine handmaid, and remember me, and not forget thine handmaid, but wilt give unto thine handmaid a man child, then I will give him unto the LORD all the days of his life, and there shall no razor come upon his head." 1 Samuel 1:10-11

What was Hannah Praying for?

Hannah was praying in bitterness of soul and spirit so that she could have a son.

Background Information about Hannah

Hannah was one of two wives married to a man named Elkenah. Although polygamy was permissible at that time under the Law of Moses, it was not an ideal situation for any woman to be in. The stresses on Hannah's marital relationship with her husband and his other wife are evident in the first chapter of 1 Samuel. Hannah was constantly harassed and provoked by the other woman, Peninnah, about her inability to have children. We learn a great deal about Hannah's character, because, despite being provoked so much, we never see her responding in a negative or confrontational way to anyone. Most people fight back when they are personally attacked, but Hannah did not. She chose the high road of prayer as her weapon of defense. Can you imagine what it must have been like to be in her situation? First, she was sharing her husband with another woman who was arrogant, spiteful and full of pride.

Second, although her husband apparently loved her very much, (as evidenced by his giving her a double portion to offer the Lord at the temple) she could not provide him with children. This must have been devastating to her because not being able to bear children during the time she lived in was often thought of as a curse. By her own admission in 1 Samuel 1:15, she was a woman deeply troubled. 1 Samuel 1:8 says that she was depressed and even refused to eat at times. It was obvious to everyone that not being able to have a child was a tremendous problem in her life.

We know that despite her inability to have a child after many years, Hannah remained a devout believer in God. When others may have given up praying to God or would have become bitter against God, 1 Samuel 1:3 explains that she continued to go up to Shiloh year after year to worship and make her offerings. Although she didn't receive an answer to her prayer for years, she continued to have faith that God was going to answer her prayers, as evidenced by the fact that she continued to worship and serve God as if he would answer her.

It is important to understand that Hannah experienced bitterness, but she did not become a bitter person. She never allowed her emotions to push her towards making regrettable decisions. The emotional trauma she experienced only served to motivate her more to prayer. The final prayer she made at the temple was the result of many years enduring painful insults from her husband's second wife and bitter rival, Peninnah, and from the frustration that came from years of seemingly unanswered prayers for a child. When she could not take it anymore, Hannah decided to take the next logical step when it seems like prayer is not being answered; she changed her prayer.

Key Elements of Hannah's Prayer

1. *Hannah was being provoked by her rival and made her prayer in bitterness of soul.* The fact that Hannah was constantly being provoked caused an emotional reaction in her. However, this woman of God responded in a positive, rather than negative way. She chose to fight back using the divine weapon of prayer rather than a sharp tongue or getting into a physical altercation. Many people resort to arguing with others and letting their disagreements turn physical because they lack the crucial experience of how to deal with problems in a spiritual way.

The wise person knows that not every problem in the natural world has a natural solution. Sometimes we need to look to the spiritual world for the solution, and this was the case with Hannah. In verse 1:6 we read that the Lord had closed her womb. There was nothing physical about her problem. According to the Bible, this was the Lord's doing. No matter how many fertility treatments, potions, advice, medical treatments or consultations she received, nothing was ever going to work until she received divine intervention. By understanding that the same God who caused her problem was the one who was going to fix it, she was well on her way to receiving the answer to her prayer.

2. *Hannah made her prayer at the Temple – (The House of God)*
   The house of God has always been associated with God meeting mankind in prayer. Jesus reaffirmed this in Matthew 21:13 by saying that the temple was called "the house of prayer." First and foremost, the churches and places where we worship God should be respectfully looked upon as places of prayer. Referring to the temple with the familiar word "house" gives it a familiar and comforting feeling. It helps us know that our places of worship should be viewed as homes where the people of God should feel free to discuss their thoughts and issues with their heavenly father. For Hannah, the temple was the place where she could meet with God and where he could

meet with her. We should look at our churches the same way. By making her prayer at the temple, as opposed to in her home, she was using it exactly the way God intended: as a place of worship and divine communion. A house is meant to be a place of rest, relaxation and refuge. This is what the house of God is supposed to be for us in a spiritual sense because God's name, presence, and power rests and dwell specifically in the house of God.

"And the LORD said unto him, I have heard thy prayer and thy supplication that thou hast made before me: I have hallowed this house, which thou hast built, to put my name there forever; and mine eyes and mine heart shall be there perpetually." 1 Kings 9:3

The important thing to understand about the house of God is that it is more than wood, mortar and stones. It is the place where God has put his name and represents his power, authority and presence. His eyes are in his house constantly to see everyone who comes to make prayer. His heart is there constantly to *feel* the emotion of anyone who comes make prayer. When Hannah came to pray for a child, God not only saw her, but he *felt* her need. He felt the bitterness of her soul and was determined to give her not just a son, but also one of Israel's greatest son's and prophets—Samuel.

When God is not answering our prayers, we

should look not only at how we are praying but *at where* we are praying. Where we are praying has just as much to do with how and what we pray since the house of God is supposed to be designated as the house of prayer. Not using the church for prayer is akin to having a car and choosing to walk rather than drive. Praying at home and other places is fine, but as Christians, we have to make better use of the church when we pray since it is the place where God has chosen to meet his people and we can expect to have better results. When it comes to prayer, you can walk in the spirit, run, or drive. Which do you prefer?

3. *Hannah vows to give her child to the Lord and make him a Nazarite.* Although Hannah's prayer focused on her personal needs, her prayer was not selfish because she vowed to give up the very son that she was praying for. How many of us would ask the Lord to bless us with something so that we can give it all back to him? To the normal person, this doesn't make sense. Many of us pray for financial blessings, promising to give God back ten, twenty or even thirty percent. Hannah's prayer was different in that she pledged to give *one hundred percent* of her request back to God. She did this knowing that she would only have a precious few years to wean the child before she would have to surrender him to the service of the Lord in the temple. To Hannah, a few years would be better than nothing at all.

Hannah's pledge was important because it filled

two very important needs at that time. First, Hannah wanted a son to fulfill her personal desires to have a child and be a mother. It would also put an end to the stressful situation she had to deal with on a daily basis with Peninnah. Secondly, the Lord needed another man of God to be able to minister to his people and succeed the elderly head priest, Eli. At that time, Eli had two sons who were notoriously corrupt and scandalous. After Samuel was born, he was sent to serve at the temple. According to 1 Samuel 2:12, Eli's sons were wicked and had no regard for the Lord. They stole from the offerings that people brought and fornicated with women who served at the tabernacle. Their sin and blasphemy was so great that God decided to kill them. Meanwhile, Samuel was ministering before the Lord and grew in stature and favor with God and men.

God knew what the future was going to bring and had chosen Hannah to provide him with a righteous man of God—even though Hannah did not understand why she was going through her trials of not being able to have a child. We should understand that when we are going through trials in our lives, it is often because God is preparing something in us that will later on be a blessing to others. The discouragement that we are temporarily experiencing will later turn into encouragement for others if we just continue to be faithful in prayer. As a pastor, I often have to encourage people while they are undergoing difficult circumstances. However, in order for me to be there to encourage them, I needed to have overcome the difficult circumstances that I experienced earlier in my life. How can I encourage someone if I failed all of my trials and remained discouraged? By overcoming one trial, you can potentially help hundreds of people overcome their trials. So it was with Hannah. By overcoming in prayer, Hannah later bore a son who ministered to millions. Thank God for persevering in prayer!

4. *Hannah's Prayer was blessed by the man of God when she finished.* As a sign of affirmation that Hannah was indeed praying for the right thing, Eli, the man of God, blessed her prayers. Why was this significant? Well, the Bible constantly confirms the fact that God blesses prayers when more than one person agrees on the subject matter of the prayer. Two or three people agreeing on serious matters is a principle first put forth in the Old Testament and then established in the New Testament:

> *"One witness shall not rise up against a man for any iniquity, or for any sin, in any sin that he sinneth: at the mouth of two witnesses, or at the mouth of three witnesses, shall the matter be established." Deuteronomy 19:15*

Consider the words of Christ:

> *"Again I say unto you, that if two of you shall agree on earth as touching anything that they shall ask, it shall be done for them of my Father which is in heaven. For where two or three are gathered together in my name, there am I in the midst of them." Matthew 18:19-20*

When two or more people agree that, a matter is serious enough to be brought before the throne of God so that it can be established in the earth, God takes it more seriously than when one person makes the request. This is not to say that the prayers of one person are not serious enough for God to consider, because indeed, they are, but God takes the request *more* seriously when more than one person is making the request. Doesn't our government take our petitions more seriously when more than one person makes the petition? Are not lawsuits more powerful when people file class action lawsuits as a group rather than as singular individuals? The same principle applies to the prayer request that we make to God.

Result of the Prayer

Hannah gave birth to Samuel a year later and he became one the greatest prophets in the history of Israel. Not only was he a prophet, but he became the judge and the spiritual leader of the nation for many years. It can be said that the one child that Hannah bore was more significant that all the children of Peninah, Hannah's rival for many years. Not only was Hannah blessed to have Samuel, but the Lord continued to bless her with more children than she asked for. 1 Samuel 2:21 says, "The Lord visited her and she had three more sons and two more daughters." God often provides overwhelming blessings when answering our prayers. Hannah went from having no children to probably having to hire a nanny to help her with the five she had at home and the one at the temple! Psalm 23:5 comes to my mind when I think about Hannah's situation with her rival.

"Thou preparest a table before me in the <u>presence of mine enemies</u>: thou anointest my head with oil; <u>my cup runneth over</u>. Surely goodness and mercy shall follow me all the days of my life: and I will dwell in the house of the LORD forever." Psalm 23:5-6

Hannah was living with her enemy but God gave her the peace of mind and strength to be able to endure the constant harassment and humiliation. Although the answer to her prayer was not immediate, God's anointing, goodness and mercy were so plentiful that she could coexist peacefully with her enemy. Over the next few years, the Lord provided an overwhelming blessing of five more children. Her cup ran over with more than what she could ever dream of. This was God's goodness and mercy following her throughout the rest of her life. Faithfulness in prayer will bring overwhelming blessing every time!

2

HEZEKIAH'S PRAYER FOR HEALING

The Prayer

"I beseech thee, O LORD, remember now how I have walked before thee in truth and with a perfect heart, and have done that which is good in thy sight. And Hezekiah wept sore." 2 Kings 20:3

What was Hezekiah Praying for?

Hezekiah was praying to be healed of a boil. This boil had brought upon a sickness that was going to cause him to die.

Background Information about Hezekiah

Hezekiah was king of Judah and a very godly man. When we look at the life of Hezekiah, we see that he was no stranger to prayer and doing God's will. 2 Chronicles 31:20 says that everything Hezekiah did throughout Judah was good, right and faithful before the Lord. This means that he was righteous in the sight of God and to those who knew him. 2 Chronicles 31:21 continues with how he sought God and worked wholeheartedly in everything that he undertook in the service of God's temple and in obedience to the law and commandments. In the first month of his reign he purified the temple by removing everything that was defiled or unclean. (2 Chronicles 31:29). In 2 Chronicles 31:4-7, we read that Hezekiah restored celebrations, feast offerings and called on the people of Judah to return to the Lord. He ordered the Israelites to bring tithes and offerings in accordance to the Old Testament law to support the temple and priests. He destroyed the high places and restored worship at the temple. All of these activities show that he valued his role as a spiritual leader just as much as being a political leader. Because of all of the good deeds he did in God's sight, he prospered greatly.

Hezekiah had already made a great prayer to God and received miraculous deliverance from Sennecherib, the king of Assyria, as described in 2 Chronicles 32:1-22. After this great victory, 2 Chronicles 32:23 says that many brought gifts unto the Lord in Jerusalem. Hezekiah was magnified in the sight of all nations from that point. He had everything a person could dream of before sickness suddenly came upon him: wealth, power and a fantastic relationship with the Lord. When Isaiah the prophet came to tell him to set his house in order because he was going to die, it would have seemed as if he had lost everything that was important to him in this world.

Key Elements of Hezekiah's prayer

1. *Hezekiah reminded God of everything good that he had done.*
Some say that our works do not matter because God
justifies and saves us by faith alone. This is simply not
true. James says this concerning faith:

*"Even so faith, if it hath not works, is dead, being alone. Yea, a
man may say, Thou hast faith, and I have works: shew me thy faith
without thy works, and I will shew thee my faith by my works."*
James 2:17

When Hezekiah became sick and knew that he was going
to die, he wisely reminded God about the works he had
done in his life. Hezekiah was known for his steadfast
righteousness when facing trials in his life. He did not
allow himself to bow to political pressure but stood
steadfast and unwavering in his commitment to make all
of Judah godly again. As a king, Hezekiah led
reformations in his country to restore the true worship of
God, so everyone knew what he stood for. When faced
with invasion, he told his people not to trust in military
numbers but to trust in God to deliver them. (2
Chronicles 32:6-8) This was something no one could
deny. No one could deny that Hezekiah trusted in God.
When he prayed to be healed, God remembered his
righteousness. He let God know that he deserved to
continue living because he was an example of
righteousness to others.

Having been in this situation myself, I know that
Hezekiah told the Lord that if he extended his life, he
would not only continue to exalt the name of the Lord, as

23

he had in the past, but that he would do even more for God because of his great mercy. How could God refuse such a bargain? Hezekiah had already proved himself righteous, so God knew that he would keep his oath and give him more glory, praise and honor in the sight of men.

2. *Hezekiah humbled himself to make his prayer.* After everything he had done for God, Hezekiah could have become frustrated and bitter because God allowed him to become sick. As someone who has dedicated his life to serving God, and experienced a life threatening sickness, I can relate to Hezekiah's situation. I know the humiliation and distress that comes from being a man of God stricken with sickness. Those who do not believe in God mock you with lies that God, who is supposed to have everything in control, could not control your sickness. Those who at one time believed in you now have doubts because they see that your life and everything you have done is now in jeopardy. Others may wonder about you as a leader because foresaw things before they happened in others lives, but you did not foresee your own trial.

As a leader, this can be an extremely frustrating test of your faith. Everything, especially your very life is at stake if God does not heal you. Either God heals you and you live, or you die and your legacy is finished. Most people choose to give up on God at this point. However, here we see Hezekiah's display of great faith by offering up one last prayer. This was what many would consider a "Hail

24

Mary" prayer to see if God would answer. It worked because Hezekiah's continued faith showed that he trusted God and did not resort to bitterness. Because of this, God answered him.

3. *Hezekiah was broken and contrite.* In 2 Kings 20:30, it tells us that Hezekiah "wept bitterly". He had no shame in letting out all of his emotions and concerns. On one's deathbed, most people have a tendency to get honest about everything they have done and who they are. The deathbed is no place to hide things from God and Hezekiah used his last opportunity to plead his case to God for an extension on his life. God loves when people are completely open, honest and emotional with him in regard to their present state.

The psalmist says this:

"The LORD is nigh unto them that are of a broken heart; and saveth such as be of a contrite spirit." Psalm 34:18

The heart that is broken and contrite draws the Spirit of God to it because it no longer has pride, guile or stubbornness residing within it anymore. Because of this, it is now easy for the Lord to penetrate and work. Anything that once stood against God has spilled out through every broken area of the heart and now God can finally get through and have his way. When the stony wall of our heart is broken down, the Lord can enter and do the wonderful and miraculous things that he has always wanted to do. Hezekiah's situation allowed a completely open and honest dialogue with God that was sure to be answered.

Result of Hezekiah's Prayer

This prayer is great for several reasons. First, God reversed a previous decision he had made about letting Hezekiah die. The Lord spoke to the prophet Isaiah and instructed him to turn around, go back to the king and tell him that he would not only be healed, but would have fifteen additional years of life added. (2 Kings 20:4-6)

Second, God does another great miracle by turning the shadow of the sun dial back ten degrees as a sign that Hezekiah would be healed. (2 Kings 20:8-10) An interesting note about Hezekiah's miraculous healing was that God did not simply make the sickness disappear, but rather he had the prophet Isaiah give him a *prescription* through which he would be healed. This shows us that God does sometimes performs miraculous healings through the marvels of modern science. God can directly heal someone without intervening through men, or he may choose to work through people. God chose to work through men in Hezekiah's case in the form of lump of figs that was placed on the boil that had caused his sickness. (2 Kings 20:7)

3

JESUS' PRAYER IN GETHSEMANE

The Prayer

"And he came out, and went, as he was wont, to the Mount of Olives; and his disciples also followed him. And when he was at the place, he said unto them, pray that ye enter not into temptation. And he was withdrawn from them about a stone's cast, and kneeled down, and prayed, Saying, Father, if thou be willing, remove this cup from me: nevertheless not my will, but thine, be done. And there appeared an angel unto him from heaven, strengthening him. And being in an agony he prayed more earnestly: and his sweat was as it were great drops of blood falling down to the ground." Luke 22:41-44

What was Jesus Praying for?

The cause of Jesus' prayer is illustrated in what he said to his disciples. Jesus spoke to them as a father giving a lesson to his children. He taught them that prayer is necessary to keep one from entering into temptation. This was the eve of the greatest event in human history and Jesus was praying so that he would not "enter into temptation." Jesus needed to pray in order to ensure that no aspect of his humanity would cause the deity inside of him to avoid going to the cross and dying for the sins of mankind. Matthew 26:41 gives a similar account of this prayer and adds: "The spirit indeed is willing, but the flesh is weak."

The spirit inside of Jesus had perfect intentions of going to the cross, but the flesh did not want to. How do we know this? Jesus asked the Father in Luke 24:42 if it is possible to take the burden of having to go to the cross away from him. We see just how important this prayer really was because Jesus chose to do the will of God rather than his own personal will by saying, "nevertheless, not my will, but thine, be done." From this, we clearly see the power of prayer to bring about the necessary submission to accomplish God's will in our life when we take the time to bring our burdens to the Father as Jesus did.

Background Information about Jesus' Prayer in Gethsemane

The prayer in Gethsemane followed the last meal that Jesus had with his disciples. The disciples were unaware that Jesus would be arrested, tried and crucified in the coming hours. Jesus knew that very shortly he would be betrayed by Judas Iscariot, turned over to the Jewish leaders and crucified the next day. The emotional pain of betrayal, the physical agony of the cross and the crushing burden of mankind's sins, would certainly have been weighing heavily on Jesus's mind at this time. Without prayer, no one could imagine, much less actually go through with the events that were soon to proceed. Matthew 26:37 states that Jesus was sorrowful and his soul was very heavy. And who wouldn't be under these circumstances? This was his moment and he was not going to disappoint the Father, himself, or mankind. In order for Him to go to the cross, he had to go to Gethsemane first and make this prayer.

John the Baptist called him the Lamb of God who was come to take away the sin of the world. Jesus knew that the one purpose he had come into the world for was now at hand. (John 1:29) Like us, Jesus had friends, loved ones and acquaintances that he had grown to love and did not want to leave. Few people who know that they are going to die willingly allow it to happen. This is why Jesus needed something supernatural to help him make it to the cross. For Him, prayer was not just an option at this time, it was a necessity. This prayer at Gethsemane propelled Him toward the cross, rather than away from it. Jesus showed us that prayer is the necessary component which compels us to go forward towards God's will, especially when we are resisting it. Prayer is necessary at those key moments when we are trying to decide to accept or reject God's plan for us. Prayer changes our heart from being tempted to giving in to the weakness of flesh to following the desire of the willing spirit.

Key Elements of Jesus' Prayer

1. *Jesus withdrew from others to make his prayer.* There's a time and a place to pray with others and there's a time when we must petition God for our needs alone. Jesus brought several disciples along not to help him, but to watch him pray so that they would learn what he was doing. After his

29

arrival at Gethsemane, Jesus intentionally withdrew himself a stone's throw away. He understood that this prayer was to be about his humanity wrestling with the deity inside of him and the deity could not lose. At this point, there was too much at stake for him to be distracted by late night weariness and complaints. Everyone, including Jesus, was tired but Jesus had to somehow summon supernatural strength to pray. To endure the cross he would need to be at his strongest, even though he was now at his weakest. His decision to pray alone is reminiscent of what he taught the disciples during the Sermon on the Mount:

"But thou, when thou prayest, enter into thy closet, and when thou hast shut thy door, pray to thy Father which is in secret; and thy Father which seeth in secret shall reward thee openly." Matthew 6:6

Like Jacob wresting at Peniel, humanity needed to once again wrestle with deity for a people to survive. Jesus had no intention of losing this showdown. He could not afford distractions and needed to pray alone.

2. *Jesus admitted his weaknesses.* While it may be hard to imagine Jesus as having any weaknesses, the human side of him did. However, the wisdom of Christ was to acknowledge, admit and deal with it head-on rather than ignore it. Pride would have overlooked the weakness of his flesh and could have quite possibly caused him to overlook the cross. Rather than overlooking the weakness of his human flesh, Jesus wisely leaned on the strength of his divine spirit and brought himself to a place of prayer

where the weakness could be dealt with properly. It is extremely important to deal with any weaknesses that we may have by presenting them to God to deal with.

"Confess your faults one to another, and pray one for another, that ye may be healed. The effectual fervent prayer of a righteous man availeth much." James 5:16

The only way to deal with our faults is to acknowledge them and not try to cover them up. Acknowledging and dealing with faults (or "a" fault) allows them to be healed and allows our prayers to be both effective and prevailing. Many people see acknowledging weaknesses as a fault. The only true fault is that we don't admit our weaknesses and allow God to deal with them. A weakness that's not acknowledged can never be dealt with and will always be a hindrance to prayer. This leads to interference in getting God's will done. Jesus willingly admitted that he did not want to go to the cross in prayer. The Holy Spirit was able to persuade the human part of him to let God's will be done and go forward to the cross even though the spiritual part of him did want to do it. His decision to follow God's will was a direct result of prayer. I shudder to imagine what would have happened if our Lord had not made this prayer.

3. *Jesus prayed with everything that he had.* Many people fear getting too emotional when they pray but prayer is all about emotion. Prayer is not a time to be reserved. It's a time to bare everything inside our body, mind, soul and

spirit before our Creator. The scriptures tell us this:

"Hear, O Israel: The LORD our God is one LORD: And thou shalt love the LORD thy God with all thine heart, and with all thy soul, and with all thy might." Deuteronomy 6:4-5

Jesus reiterated this commandment in the New Testament, saying that it was the greatest commandment.

"Master, which is the great commandment in the law? Jesus said unto him, Thou shalt love the Lord thy God with all thy heart, and with all thy soul, and with all thy mind. This is the first and great commandment." Matthew 22:36-38

If the greatest commandment is to love God with all of our heart, soul, mind and strength, then why don't we open up and show our affection with everything that we have? The prayer that Jesus made in Gethsemane was emotional, visceral and physical. The Greek meaning of the word Gethsemane means "oil press." Gethsemane was a place for crushing and grinding olives. Gethsemane was an emotionally grinding and crushing place for Christ. Some prayers that will only come forth when our body and spirit has been crushed so that the sweet oil of prayer can be released. Every prayer does not have to be like this, but great prayers do. With the sin of mankind on his shoulders and the outcome of eternity depending on this prayer, Jesus needed to summon every ounce of physical and emotional strength he could muster that late night.

So important was the success of Jesus' prayer that an angel appeared to strengthen him as he was praying. (Luke 22:43) While he didn't specifically ask for angelic help, God saw the effort that was being put forth and gave him help. We should understand that when God sees us giving everything we have in prayer, he will match our efforts and give us his best. If we pray mundane prayers, then we should expect mundane results. If we pray exceptional prayers, then we should expect exceptional results. In Luke 22:44, Luke wrote that Jesus prayed even more earnestly. Jesus did not allow himself the comfort of believing that his prayer had been answered just because an angel had appeared. No, he turned up the intensity and became *even more determined* when he saw that he now had God's attention. Most of us would have stopped praying the moment an angel appeared, but not Christ. He ignored the angel because he was so focused on his goal of receiving the necessary strength to go the cross for us. His intensity increased until sweat poured down from his face as blood falling to the ground. For him, this was more than prayer. It was more than communication with the Father. It was a wrestling match for the souls of mankind and he was not going to lose. Jesus was wrestling with Satan to free the souls of all mankind from the burden of sin and to bring us back into fellowship with the Creator.

When serious issues are on the line, such as the burden of souls, we have to be ready for the physical and emotional exertion that this kind of prayer brings. To deliver souls from the clutches of Satan we often have to break strongholds and chains of sin that are binding them. Jesus tells us that in order to save and heal those hindered by Satan we must first bind the enemy:

"But if I cast out devils by the Spirit of God, then the kingdom of God is come unto you. Or else how can one enter into a strong man's house, and spoil his goods, except he first bind the strong man? And then he will spoil his house." Matthew12:28-29

If you want to save one person, let alone the entire world, you have to prepare to fight the one that has control over them. Jesus understood this and wrestled in prayer to bind Satan and free our souls.

4. *Jesus was praying for others and not himself.* Arguably the greatest prayers in the bible are those that have been prayed for someone else. This is because of selflessness. It's very easy to pray for ourselves, especially when we are in need or greatly desire something. It's an entirely different matter to pray for the needs of someone else. The unique aspect of Jesus' prayer is not only that he was praying for others, but that he was praying for others that had no concern for him. In fact, many of those for whom he was praying sought his harm and wanted to see him tortured and crucified. This however, did not faze Jesus. He had taught his disciples to pray for those who disliked them.

"But I say unto you, Love your enemies, bless them that curse you, do good to them that hate you, <u>and pray for them which despitefully use you, and persecute you;</u>" Matthew 5:44

Not only is this difficult for most people but I would even dare to say it is downright unnatural! Despite this difficulty, Matthew goes on to say that this is the type of prayer that impresses God the most.

"That ye may be the children of your Father which is in heaven: for he maketh his sun to rise on the evil and the good, and sendeth rain on the just and on the unjust. For if ye love them which love you, what reward have ye? do not even the publicans the same?"
Matthew 5:45-46

Result of the Prayer

The great prayer that Jesus made delivered the souls of all mankind. If we want to accept his free gift of salvation, then we must do it through repentance and water baptism. (Read Mark 16:15-16 and Acts 2:38) Although it was grueling and he suffered more than anyone in human history did, he made it to the cross. He was crucified and rose from the dead on the third day to give us hope for the resurrection. In my opinion, no greater prayer has been prayed and no greater result has been achieved than what Christ began in Gethsemane and finished on the cross.

4

JOSHUA'S PRAYER FOR THE SUN AND MOON TO STAND STILL

The Prayer

"Then spake Joshua to the LORD in the day when the LORD delivered up the Amorites before the children of Israel, and he said in the sight of Israel, Sun, stand thou still upon Gibeon; and thou, Moon, in the valley of Ajalon. And the sun stood still, and the moon stayed, until the people had avenged themselves upon their enemies. Is not this written in the book of Jasher? So the sun stood still in the midst of heaven, and hasted not to go down about a whole day." Joshua 10:12-13

What was Joshua Praying for?

Joshua was pursuing a coalition of enemy kings who had attacked Gibeonite allies under Israelite protection. Because he didn't want the enemy to get away and have to fight them again, Joshua prayed so that he could continue pursuing his enemies. *persistente*

Background information about Joshua

Joshua left Egypt with Moses and the rest of the Israelites. Over the years, Joshua rose to become Moses' minister. Joshua and Caleb were the only two out of twelve men who had spied out the Promised Land who believed that God could deliver the land to them. Because only ~~ten~~ two out of the twelve spies believed that the Lord could deliver Promised Land to Israelites, the entire nation had to wait forty years to enter and begin the conquest of the land that would one day be theirs. By the time this battle had come, Joshua was a hardened man of war intent on finishing the conquest he had begun years earlier. Joshua had waited forty years to enter the Promised Land. He had fought numerous battles against walled cities like Jericho. He had battled giants like Og of Sihon, and was constantly outnumbered and outmatched, yet God still gave him victory. By this time in his life, Joshua was eager to conquer the land and not let the enemy slip away.

Key Elements of Joshua's Prayer

1. *Joshua understood what God's desires for his people were at that time.* It was at this particular time that God promised the Israelites that they would inherit the land of Canaan and that he would drive out the people who currently lived there. The promise had been made to Abraham almost five hundred years earlier (See Genesis 15:13-21) and to Moses more than forty years earlier. (Exodus 3:8) It was

again confirmed to Joshua, as seen in Joshua 1:1-7.

Now the time was at hand and God instructed Joshua to conquer the land and not to leave anyone alive. This was a harsh thing to do and other Jewish leaders like Saul could not bring themselves to do it,(1 Samuel 15) but Joshua had set in his heart to do everything that the Lord had spoken him to him. He also did not want to have to fight the same enemy again later. This is why he asked for God's help to finish what he had started. By praying this prayer, Joshua was practically guaranteed success, even though it seemed near impossible, because it was directly in line with what God needed to be done.

2. *Joshua believed God could answer his prayer, even though it seemed impossible.* We should understand that even though something may seem impossible for God to perform and beyond the realms of natural science, if it is in line with God's promise, it then becomes possible. As humans, we sometimes limit God's power because we think that something is beyond our limited understanding of nature and science. What we have to understand is that God created the laws of science that we understand and can supersede them anytime he pleases. God caused the earth to rotate on its axis and he can cause it to stop at any time with no ill effects. It was God who mandated the earth to revolve around the sun and the moon around the earth, so he can cause any of these things to cease at his divine pleasure. The scriptures consistently tell us that nothing is

38

impossible with God:

"But Jesus beheld them, and said unto them, With men this is impossible; but with God all things are possible," Matthew 19:26

"Jesus said unto him,' If thou canst believe, all things are possible to him that believeth."' Mark 9:23

"For with God nothing shall be impossible." Luke 1:37

We should never limit God because he does not limit himself. God loves to confound those who believe that there are things that he cannot do. Why? To show that he indeed is God.

"But God hath chosen the foolish things of the world <u>to confound the wise</u>; and God hath chosen the weak things of the world to confound the things which are mighty; And base things of the world, and things which are despised, hath God chosen, yea, and things which are not, to bring to nought things that are: That no flesh should glory in his presence." 1 Corinthians 1:27-29

By the time God was finished answering Joshua's prayers, the writer says that there had never been a day like it before, not until this day. This means that it superseded all the prayers of Noah, Abraham, Isaac, Jacob and even Moses. Joshua dared to pray the greatest prayer ever and God met and answered him according to his faith. As the scriptures says:

"Then touched he their eyes, saying, According to your faith be it

unto you." Matthew 9:29

If we dare to stretch our faith and pray great prayers, then God *will* dare to answer them. I can personally testify to God's power in this way. One day when I was sick in the hospital and began bleeding and losing a great deal of blood from Ulcerative Colitis, the alarms on the monitor sounded and the nurse came running into the room because she thought I was dying. She took my blood pressure and said that it was physically impossible for me to be alive because the pressure was so low that there was no natural way that my heart could be still pumping blood throughout my body. I looked at the nurse and smiled because I felt the warm anointing presence of God all over me and knew he had went beyond science to keep me alive. I can tell you there is *nothing* impossible with God if you only believe.

Result of the Prayer

As a result of his prayer, the sun remained in the same place for the entire day and the Israelites were able to defeat the armies that had come out to fight against them. Joshua also captured and killed the five kings who were the leaders of the enemy armies. Because of this great victory the children of Israel removed a major obstacle to achieving their goal of conquering the Promised Land and fulfilling their destiny. Joshua 10:14 gives us more information about the impressive results of Joshua's prayer:

"And there was no day like that before it or after it, that the

LORD *hearkened unto the voice of a man: for the LORD fought for Israel." Joshua 10:14*

One of the reasons why this prayer was selected as one of the ten greatest prayers of the Bible is because it was said that there was never a day before or after when God listened to one man's prayer and fought for him. This shows the power that just one praying person can have. It also validates the power of James 5:16 where it says, "the effectual fervent prayer of a righteous man availeth much." Never underestimate the power that one righteous person has with God!

5

Solomon's Prayer for Wisdom

The Prayer

"In Gibeon the LORD appeared to Solomon in a dream by night: and God said, Ask what I shall give thee. And Solomon said, Thou hast shewed unto thy servant David my father great mercy, according as he walked before thee in truth, and in righteousness, and in uprightness of heart with thee; and thou hast kept for him this great kindness, that thou hast given him a son to sit on his throne, as it is this day. And now, O LORD my God, thou hast made thy servant king instead of David my father: and I am but a little child: I know not how to go out or come in. And thy servant is in the midst of thy people which thou hast chosen, a great people, that cannot be numbered nor counted for multitude. Give therefore thy servant an understanding heart to judge thy people that I may discern between good and bad: for who is able to judge this thy so great a people?" 1 Kings 3:5-9

What was Solomon Praying for?

Solomon was asking God specifically to give him the wisdom and understanding to rule over the kingdom of Israel which had been left to him by his father, David. He wanted to have an understanding heart that would allow him to know the difference between good and evil. He realized the importance of being able to make good and righteous decisions as a leader. This desire is something that separated Solomon from many other kings of Israel and Judah. His desire for more wisdom caused him to ask God for more. This is very interesting because 1 Kings 2:8 said that Solomon already possessed a fair amount of wisdom because David called him "a man of wisdom." Solomon's continued pursuit of wisdom is also evident throughout the book of Ecclesiastes. When asked by God what he required in 1 Kings chapter 3, Solomon humbled himself before the Lord and behaved as a child with no wisdom, showing the Lord his thirst for wisdom and understanding.

Background information about Solomon

When Solomon made his prayer for wisdom he had just become king after a struggle for the throne. His succession to the throne was not easy because he had been challenged by his brothers, his father's former military commander, Joab, and Abiather the priest. After a bit of shrewd maneuvering by Solomon and his mother, he was finally announced as the legitimate heir to the throne by his father David. Solomon was motivated by two things.

First, he wanted to keep the charge that his father David had given him to become a good king and continue the great legacy that David had begun. Second, Solomon craved wisdom and understanding. He knew that he could achieve all of his goals in life with God given wisdom, so this is what he asked for. By asking for wisdom he showed great wisdom!

After he became king, Solomon realized that obtaining the throne was one thing, and holding onto it and becoming a great king, was something else. This realization must have definitely factored into his decision to ask God to give him wisdom. Like King Hezekiah, another great biblical king known for his prayers, Solomon was a righteous man from his youth and sought to please the Lord with great sacrifices and offerings at the house of God. He made sure that everyone knew where he stood when it came to his religious lifestyle and convictions. By the time God appeared to him at Gibeon, he already had a track record of outstanding dedication and service to God, so it was no wonder that God appeared to him in a dream to present him with a gift.

Key Elements of Solomon's Prayer

1. *God appeared to Solomon even though there were still some things in his life that were not entirely perfect.*1 Kings Chapter three starts out by telling us all about Solomon's activities. Verse two starts out with the phrase: "only the people still sacrificed in high places because there was no house of the Lord." This is meant to give us the impression that everything else Solomon was doing was okay, except for this one little thing. The writer even seems to make a bit of an excuse for Solomon by saying that the people were doing this because there was no official house of God for them to worship in while the new temple was being built.

From this inference, we can see that by allowing the people to continue their sacrifices in high places, Solomon was turning a blind eye to something that he knew was not acceptable to God.

In various places in the Old Testament such as Numbers 33:52, 1Kings 14:23, 1 Kings 15:14 and 1 Kings 22:43, we find that God did not like the pagan practice of making sacrifices in high places. This was a Canaanite ritual that God ordered to be stopped when the children of Israel entered into the Promised Land but continued to be practiced. Solomon should have known better, but apparently God let this one thing slide and still spoke blessings into his life. This was because Solomon was making a great effort to be righteous and achieve wisdom and understanding. From this we can learn that God can still answer our prayers and bless us if we are not perfect, but making a serious effort to get there.

2. *Solomon humbled himself.* When his father, David, had given Solomon instructions on his deathbed, he acknowledged that Solomon was already wise. (1 Kings 2:9) Despite this, when the Lord appeared to him, he asked for wisdom saying that he was "but a little child." By uplifting God and debasing himself, Solomon was showing humility in the sight of God. Humility is a key element of prayer, especially when being in the direct presence of God. When you are in the presence of God you must realize that whoever you think you are, and no matter what you

think you possess, God is greater than you and he always has something more he can add to your life. Solomon wisely humbled himself so that God could lift him up.

3. *Solomon took the time to seek God.* As the king of Israel, Solomon was undoubtedly very busy and could have made many excuses for not seeking the Lord. He wisely realized that everything he possessed came from God and everything that he wanted to possess would come from God. Solomon was one of the few kings of Israel (and later Judah) who was wholly righteous and set his heart to serve God. Even today you rarely see leaders of nations and political leaders publicly acknowledge and serve God. Solomon was unique in his acknowledgment of God and as a result God richly blessed him for it.

4. *Solomon acknowledged what God had done for his father David.* In 1 Kings 3:6, the first thing Solomon did when God appeared to him was acknowledge everything that he had done for his father, David. Solomon was king because God made a promise to keep David's descendants on the throne throughout the generations. By acknowledging this, Solomon showed his appreciation for what God had done for him and his family.

5. *Solomon's request was unselfish because he asked for an understanding heart so that he could lead.* How many people would ask for wisdom and discernment if God allowed them to have anything that they wanted? Once again, Solomon showed his wisdom by asking for something that would allow him to be the best leader he could be for

God's people and not for himself. His decision showed God that his desire to rule over God's people was not just for selfish reasons. Those who lead God's people should realize that when God puts someone in a position of leadership, he put them there as shepherds over God's flock. When a leader comes to this conclusion, not only can God use them more to accomplish his divine purposes, but they will also receive greater honor and glory from others.

"And I will give you pastors according to mine heart, which shall feed you with knowledge and understanding." Jeremiah 3:15

God's chooses leaders who will pastor *his* people and who will feed *his* people with knowledge and understanding. Only when leaders acknowledge that God has put them in their leadership role does he equip them so that they can be effective as God wants them to be. In addition, God's people will get the knowledge and understanding that they need. Solomon wanted to be able to make good decisions and know *good from evil*. This way he could understand the many complex situations that he encountered as the king of Israel. He didn't want to make poor decisions or govern from selfishness, pride, greed and arrogance.

Asking God to properly equip him with understanding and discernment allowed Solomon to acquire the proper skills to be a good leader. This also proved that he had the prerequisite amount of wisdom necessary to be blessed with additional gifts from God.

This vast amount of wisdom allowed him to become the *world's greatest* leader, rather that just a great leader of Israel.

6. *God spoke to Solomon in a dream.* Perhaps the most intriguing aspect of Solomon's prayer is the fact that it occurred within a dream. Most prayers and contact with God are made in a lucid and conscious state, but God chose to contact Solomon through a dream. The Bible contains many occurrences where God has spoken to someone either directly or indirectly through dreams.

Some examples of God speaking to kings indirectly through a dream about the future are:
a. Genesis chapter 40 - Pharaoh's dream about seven lean and seven fat cattle.
b. Daniel chapter 2 - Nebuchadnezzar's dream about the large image of gold, silver, bronze, iron and clay.

Examples of God speaking directly to someone in a dream:
a. Matthew 1 - God warns Joseph in a dream to flee with Jesus to Egypt in order to escape Herod's order to kill firstborn children.
b. Matthew chapter 2 - God warns all of the wise men who had come to see Jesus not to return to see Herod.
c. Matthew chapter 27 - God warns Pontius Pilate's wife not to have

anything to do with the trial of Jesus because she had suffered many things that day in a dream because of Jesus.

The question remains, why does God speak to people, especially kings and heads of state like Pharaoh, Nebuchadnezzar and Solomon in dreams rather than appearing to them openly? The answer lies in Job 33:15:

"For God speaketh once, yea twice, yet man perceiveth it not. In a dream, in a vision of the night, when deep sleep falleth upon men, in slumberings upon the bed; Then he openeth the ears of men, and sealeth their instruction, That he may withdraw man from his purpose, and hide pride from man. He keepeth back his soul from the pit, and his life from perishing by the sword." Job 33:14-18

God can speak to people a few times while they are lucid and awake but they still may not understand what he is trying to say. In a dream, God has a person's full attention and there are no other distractions, worries or concerns. When he speaks to them in a dream his words are deeply imprinted in their minds. God can give them joy or terror and his instruction will be deeply seared into their minds. In a dream, he can turn a person from whatever original purpose they had regardless of whatever amount of pride they have in order to get his message across. This is why when God needs to convey and important message to great leaders, he usually

49

chooses a dream.

It is very easy for a leader of great pride and power to ignore a warning from advisers or prophets. However, when God speaks directly to them in a dream, more times than not, they will be convinced. God spoke this way often to godly and ungodly leaders in the Bible. By speaking to Solomon in a dream, God had his undivided attention and made an impression upon Solomon that he would not soon forget.

The Result of Solomon's Prayer

God was more impressed with what Solomon had *not* asked for than what he *did* ask for. He let Solomon know that since he had not asked for selfish things, such as long life, riches or the lives of his enemies, he would bless him with more than what he originally asked for. Since he had only asked for understanding and the ability to discern judgment, God gave him the things that he had not asked for in addition. It is so crucial to understand that there is nothing wrong with praying for the things that we want or need but God is greatly impressed when we pray for the things that the people we influence want or need. Look at what the key portions of the Lord's Prayer in Matthew chapter six says about prayer:

"Be not ye therefore like unto them: for your Father knoweth what things ye have need of, before ye ask him. After this manner therefore pray ye:

50

Our Father which art in heaven, Hallowed be thy name. Thy kingdom come. Thy will be done in earth, as it is in heaven." Matthew 6:8-10

God knows what our needs are before we pray. If this is the case, why is prayer necessary if God already knows what we need? Because he wants to see how *we are going to respond to what we need.* Prayer goes both ways. When praying we are often waiting to see how God is going to respond to our request, but fifty percent of our prayers are answered by *how we respond to our needs.* Are we so concerned with our own needs that we don't pray for others or for God's will to be done in the earth? By giving us instructions on how to pray, Jesus is telling us, "Yes, your Father already knows that his children have needs, but he wants you to focus on praying for his needs first, which is having his will done on earth."

God is going to take care of us as his children. We have to trust him to take care of our needs. Our main concern should be taking care of his needs first, not our own. Of course, this is difficult because we have our wants, our needs and our desires yet the daily practice of prayer is supposed to teach us how to supersede our desires with God's desires. By learning how to do this we can't be focused on self, and in the process, we will have our needs and the will of God taken care of.

Praying with this mentality worked wonderfully in Solomon's life. He asked for two things and ended up getting a whole lot more, eventually becoming the wisest and wealthiest man to have ever lived. This was because he put the needs of God and his people before his own needs. As a result, Solomon had his prayer answered and was given additional blessings. When we read about the life of Solomon, we read about a man whose life was filled with excess. Every aspect of Solomon's life was filled with God supplying more than what he needed. This is because God wanted to show the benefits of putting put God's priorities first, and our own second. God will reward us with overflowing blessings when we serve him and learn to master the delicate art of prayer. Look at these examples of God promising excess in the scriptures if we trust in him:

"Thou preparest a table before me in the presence of mine enemies: thou anointest my head with oil; my cup runneth over." Psalms 23:5

"Bring ye all the tithes into the storehouse, that there may be meat in mine house, and prove me now herewith, saith the LORD of hosts, if I will not open you the windows of heaven, and pour you out a blessing, that there shall not be room enough to receive it." Malachi 3:10

"Give, and it shall be given unto you; good measure, pressed down, and shaken together, and running over, shall men give into your bosom. For with the same measure that ye mete withal it shall be measured to you again. Luke 6:38

"Now unto him that is able to do exceeding abundantly above all that we ask or think, according to the power that worketh in us," Ephesians 3:20

God will meet exceed our needs when we put our full trust in him and do his will. When we have the faith to put his will first and ours second, he will begin doing more for us than we could ever imagine.

6

ELIJAH'S PRAYER TO TURN ISRAEL BACK TO GOD

The Prayer

"And it came to pass at the time of the offering of the evening sacrifice, that Elijah the prophet came near, and said, LORD God of Abraham, Isaac, and of Israel, let it be known this day that thou art God in Israel, and that I am thy servant, and that I have done all these things at thy word. Hear me, O LORD, hear me, that this people may know that thou art the LORD God, and that thou hast turned their heart back again." 1 Kings 18:36-37

What was Elijah Praying for?

Elijah was praying to turn Israel back toward the worshipping of the one true God. At that time, King Ahab and his wife Jezebel were leading the nation into idolatry and wickedness. In 1 Kings 18, Jezebel was hunting down prophets of the Lord to kill them. Most of the nation of Israel had stopped serving God and were worshipping Baal and other false gods. Elijah was praying to change all of this and restore the nation back to worshipping the one true God.

Background Information about Elijah

Elijah had been a prophet for some time and by now was the most hated adversary of King Ahab and Queen Jezebel. Elijah had previously prophesied to the king that it would not rain until he alone gave the word that it should. God honored his words and didn't let one drop of rain fall in Israel for three years. Elijah was one of the few men of God who had the power and courage to stand up to the wickedness of Ahab and Jezebel.

A death warrant was issued against the prophet because of his courage to stand up for God. Elijah was one of the fortunate few prophets that remained alive and God was telling him to go and show himself to Ahab in order to confront him in the sight of all Israel. Elijah went to confront him because he trusted in the power of God to protect and deliver him from any situation. He needed to reverse the tidal wave of sin and idolatry that had overtaken his nation. He believed that one man's faith and righteousness could make a difference and turn the entire country back to God.

Key Elements of Elijah's Prayer

1. *Elijah did not care that he was the only one willing*

to stand up against wickedness and idolatry. He had boldness when it came to professing his faith in God. Elijah believed that he had a mandate from God to remove spiritual idolatry from Israel and turn the nation back to serving the one true God. Luke 1:17 says that Elijah became known throughout history for turning the hearts of Israel back to serving God and preparing the way of the Lord. Not many people are willing to lay everything on the line to profess their faith in God.

Many people find it hard to even witness to the person next them on the job or sitting in the seat next to them. There often seems to be an invisible barrier of politeness, political correctness, fear and embarrassment that keeps Christians from professing their faith like they should. We are either often too afraid to tell people that they need to stand up for God and cease from sin or we tell ourselves that we are waiting for "the right time." The right time is now! What does Jesus have to say about this?

"Whosoever therefore shall be <u>ashamed</u> of me and of my words in this adulterous and sinful generation; of him also shall the Son of man be <u>ashamed</u>, when he cometh in the glory of his Father with the holy angels." Mark 8:38

What does Paul have to say about boldness?

"Be not thou therefore ashamed of the testimony of our Lord, nor of me his prisoner: but be thou partaker of the afflictions of the gospel according to the power of God..." 2 Timothy 1:8

My Christian friends, now is not the time to be afraid of witnessing and standing up for Christ and his gospel. As Christians, we must emulate him and walk without fear in the spirit of Elijah and be willing to put everything on the line to make sure that the people we have a burden for can be saved. Elijah was going to serve God even if no one else did. It was good enough that the one true God was with him. We should be even bolder than Elijah because those of us who are believers in Christ have something that Elijah didn't have—the power of the Holy Spirit inside us. Jesus told the apostles in Acts 1:8 that he would give them power to be witnesses throughout the entire world. We should use that power to be witnesses. While Elijah operated solely by faith that God would send his power down from heaven, we should be confident in the power that is already dwelling inside us through the Holy Spirit! We feel God's anointing, his presence, but why not his burden and passion to spread the good news? If Christ is indeed inside of us then we have to use his Holy Spirit to do the work that he truly wants us to do: witness and testify!

1. *Elijah had a burden for the lost.* Aside from being bold, Elijah genuinely cared about the salvation of Israel. His prayer was, "that *this people* may know that thou art the LORD God, and that thou hast turned *their heart* back again." He was not just praying for God to back him up and make him look good that day. Elijah wanted God to save his people so that they would not die in idolatry and go to hell. To have a burden for lost souls means that we want what God wants for his people and begin to know how God feels for those lost souls. His urgency to save them should become our urgency. God loves everyone on the planet, but he also sees them as saved or unsaved. These are the two states of mankind. The Old Testament prophets like Isaiah, Jeremiah, Ezekiel and Zechariah would say, "the burden of the Lord", when they prophesied. The prophet and preacher know what it's like to be under the heavy weight of God's burden and what he feels for mankind. While the less inclined to witness are always waiting on *the right timing,* those under the conviction of the Holy Ghost know that time is running out. If we want to save souls and turn people back to the Lord, we must feel God's burden for the lost.

2. *Elijah believed that God would back up what he spoke by faith.* Elijah does many things by faith alone in 1 Kings 18. God tells him in verse one to

show himself to Ahab and that he would send rain. Elijah does and everything else on his own. It was Elijah's idea to assemble the prophets of Baal and the groves at Carmel for a spiritual showdown. It was his idea to say that whoever God answered by fire would be declared the winner. It was his idea to pour four barrels of water not once, twice, but three times onto the slain bullock that was to be sacrificed. And how did God answer this brashness? By sending fire down from heaven to consume the offering, every drop of water, and all the hearts of Israel! Sometimes instead of waiting for the right timing, we need to just be bold and step out by faith to do something for God. One preacher said a wild horse is better than a stubborn mule because at least it's moving. Let's get moving people of God!

The Result of Elijah's Prayer

The main result of Elijah's prayer was that those who witnessed the fire that came down from heaven during the spiritual showdown at Mount Carmel made a decision to serve the Lord. (1 Kings 18:39) Before Elijah's miraculous display, many of them were either worshipping Baal, the gods of the groves or were too afraid to openly serve the God of Israel. God openly answered Elijah and put to shame the other so-called "prophets" and this caused the people to become bold and confident. Next, God sent rain upon Israel after three years of not having it. This fulfilled the promise that God made to Elijah when he told him to go and show himself to Ahab. Elijah and the people witnessed three great miracles in one day: fire coming down from heaven, the people turning from idolatry and the miraculous appearance of rain after three years. This was a three miracle for one prayer deal!

7

The Woman with the Issue of Blood

The Prayer

"For she said within herself, if I may but touch his garment, I shall be whole." Matthew 9:21

What was the Woman praying for?

She was praying to be healed of a chronic bleeding disorder. She emphatically believed that she would be healed if she could just touch Jesus' garment.

Background Information about the Woman

We don't know much about this amazing woman. She is unnamed and her story is mentioned three times in the gospels of Matthew 9:21-22, Mark 5:25-34 and Luke 8:43-48. This woman was healed by simply touching Jesus' clothes. In Luke chapter eight we discover that she had a bleeding disorder for twelve years and spent all of her money trying to find a cure.

There are more than a few medical symptoms that could have caused her sickness. She could have suffered from menorrhagia, which is excessive or prolonged vaginal bleeding that occurs at the regular time of the menstrual cycle. The second cause could have been metrorrhagia which is uterine bleeding at irregular intervals, particularly between the expected menstrual periods. The third cause could have been menometrorrhagia, which is the combination of the menorrhagia and metrorrhagia. Menometrorrhagia is excessive uterine bleeding, both at the usual time of menstrual periods and at other irregular intervals. The fourth possible cause of her bleeding could have been dysfunctional uterine bleeding, which is when bleeding is not caused by the normal menstrual cycle. This is the most common cause of abnormal bleeding during a woman's childbearing years. Other, less possible causes could have been pregnancy, menopause, polycystic ovary syndrome (a hormone imbalance), Pelvic Inflammatory Disease or inherited bleeding disorders such as Willebrand Disease or Hemophilia.

Mark chapter five goes further in depth by telling us that she actually grew worse from the treatments physicians prescribed her. Life must have been miserable having to endure the daily physical trauma as well as being ostracized from Jewish society. Leviticus 15:19-28 says that under the Law of Moses, any woman suffering from a bleeding disorder would be ritually unclean for seven days. This meant that no one would have been allowed to touch her or anything that she touched. All of these combined troubles would have made her financially, physically and emotionally broken. She must have been desperate with nothing left but faith in God when she saw Jesus coming down the street. She was ready for a miracle!

Key Elements of the Woman's Prayer

1. *Against all odds, this woman continued to believe in God's ability to heal her.* She dealt with this issue for twelve years and spent all of her money looking for a cure, but only got worse. On top of that, she belonged to a religion whose rules and regulations made her an outcast. Despite all of this she still believed that Jesus would heal her if she could just touch his clothes. Many people would have given up and become bitter after a few months or years without God answering their prayer. For twelve long years she continued to seek after a cure and never doubted the fact that she would either find a cure or that God would heal her. The fact that she sought both medical and spiritual solutions shows that she was not fully convinced that either would work or that she was willing to try anything. The one thing we do know for certain is that she knew that she would be cured—be it by God or man.

2. *She spent everything she had, including her faith.* This woman was willing to sacrifice anything to get better. Anyone who has ever dealt with a chronic illness is willing to spend everything and more to feel normal. This woman received a healing because when she was

financially bankrupt, she tapped her spiritual reserves and withdrew an amount of faith. Faith is the currency of heaven and is measurable. Listen to the worlds of the Apostle Paul:

"For I say, through the grace given unto me, to every man that is among you, not to think of himself more highly than he ought to think; but to think soberly, according as God hath dealt to every man the measure of faith." Romans 12:3

Jesus confirms this in the Gospels:

"Wherefore, if God so clothe the grass of the field, which today is, and tomorrow is cast into the oven, shall he not much more clothe you, O ye of little faith? Matthew 6:30

"When Jesus heard it, he marveled, and said to them that followed, Verily I say unto you, I have not found so great faith, no, not in Israel." Matthew 8:10

"And the apostles said unto the Lord, increase our faith. And the Lord said, If ye had faith as a grain of mustard seed, ye might say unto this sycamore tree, Be thou plucked up by the root, and be thou planted in the sea; and it should obey you." Luke 17:5-6

The apostles asked Jesus to *increase* the faith that they *already* had. He does not tell them everyone has the same amount of faith, but rather tells them that they only need a *small amount* of faith in order to do miraculous things. Although a person may not have great financial wealth, they can have vast amounts of faith. The wonderful thing about this is that it only takes a small amount of faith to realize a miracle! Sometimes in order for the Lord to do a miracle in our lives we have to realize that the spiritual wealth we have is far more important than our financial wealth. When conventional methods failed her, this woman sought something unconventional. Divine healing often takes place when people have no other alternative but to turn to God. This is often because people are willing put all of their faith and trust in Jesus at that point. We often remove God from the equation when there are other alternatives to solving our problems. Divine healing becomes a real possibility once we put all of our trust in God.

1. *The prayer that she made was short, sweet and to the point.* In Matthew 9:21, it tells us that the woman simply thought within herself that if she could just touch Jesus' clothes, she would be healed. She did not even say the prayer aloud and was healed. This tells us that we don't always have to made loud and grandiose prayers in order for God to hear us. Because of her social stigma, she was probably afraid to speak in public, let alone ask Jesus to touch her. The love of God met her right where she was able to go and with what she was able to do at that time. The Lord saw her shame and said, "Daughter, I know what you are thinking. I have seen your suffering and am going to heal you because of your effort." Thank God that he

meets us exactly where we are in life!

2. *Healing can take place without the man of God being aware of the person in need of a healing.* This woman's desire to be healed was so strong that she literally took power out of Jesus without his consent and into her own body to receive healing. (Mark 5:30, Luke 8:46) This is reason why I believe that this prayer must be included in the top ten. Up until that point, most people who encountered Jesus needed him to touch them in order to receive their healing. The closest someone ever came to this miraculous occurrence was the centurion who believed that his paralyzed servant would be healed if Jesus just spoke the word. (Matthew 8:5-10) No other miracles ever came close to this woman's ability to actualize a healing without speaking to or having been touched by Jesus. This shows us that the power of God is available to anyone who believes in their heart that Jesus can heal them.

3. *She needed a conduit, or point of focus in order for her healing to take place.* This woman had great faith, but she needed to manifest it through a physical object. She could have just as easily said, "If I could just see Jesus" or "If he just looks my way, I will be healed." She needed to physically touch something before the healing was *actualized*. This is not unusual. When Moses was first called by God, he had very little faith in God and himself. This is why the Lord commanded him to take the rod in his hand and use it

to do miracles. (Exodus 4:17) Acts 5:15 tells us that multitudes of sick people would be laid in the streets hoping that they could at least be touched by Peter's shadow to be healed. Acts 19:12 tells us that diseases and evil spirits departed when sick people were given handkerchiefs or aprons from the Apostle Paul. People often need something that they can physically touch in order to get their faith "over the hump" to the point where they can manifest the miracle that they believe in God for. A good example of this is located in Mark chapter nine:

"And straightway the father of the child cried out, and said with tears, Lord, I believe; help thou mine unbelief." Mark 9:24

This man was saying, "Lord I believe that you can heal my child, but I don't know what to do to make it happen." I often tell people that belief is what you know God can do in your heart and faith is what you actually do to make it happen. The power of God to heal us and do miracles is constantly all around us. We just need the necessary faith to *activate* it in order for it to manifest. To pick up where we left off in story of the man with the sick child, Jesus steps in to perform the healing:

"When Jesus saw that the people came running together, he rebuked the foul spirit, saying unto him, Thou dumb and deaf spirit, I charge thee, come out of him, and enter no

more into him. And the spirit cried, and rent him sore, and came out of him: and he was as one dead; insomuch that many said, He is dead. But Jesus took him by the hand, and lifted him up; and he arose." Mark 9:25-27

Jesus performs a miracle that the disciples were not able to. We find out why they were not able to when they asked him how he was able to do it and they were not.

"And when he was come into the house, his disciples asked him privately, why could not we cast him out? And he said unto them, This kind can come forth by nothing, but by prayer and fasting." Mark 9:28-29

The secret is revealed! Jesus tells them they that were not able to cast this particular spirit out because   they did not have *enough* faith. The good news is that if they wanted the faith that he had, which could cast out more troublesome spirits, they could obtain it by prayer and fasting. Sometimes a little extra is needed to get things done.

The Result of the Woman's Prayer

Because of her prayer, this woman was completely healed. Twelve years of suffering evaporated with one touch. She also got the attention of Jesus, who comforted her and recognized her great faith.

8

MOSES' PRAYER FOR ISRAEL

The Prayer

"And Moses besought the LORD his God, and said, LORD, why doth thy wrath wax hot against thy people, which thou hast brought forth out of the land of Egypt with great power, and with a mighty hand? Wherefore should the Egyptians speak, and say, For mischief did he bring them out, to slay them in the mountains, and to consume them from the face of the earth? Turn from thy fierce wrath, and repent of this evil against thy people. Remember Abraham, Isaac, and Israel, thy servants, to whom thou swarest by thine own self, and saidst unto them, I will multiply your seed as the stars of heaven, and all this land that I have spoken of will I give unto your seed, and they shall inherit it forever." Exodus 32:11-13

What was Moses praying for?

Moses was praying for God not to destroy the Israelite people. They were three months into their journey to the Promised Land of Canaan, and briefly stopped to camp at Mount Sinai. God invited Moses to the top of the mountain for forty days and nights to give him instructions in regard to The Ten Commandments, construction of the tabernacle, and other Jewish laws. During this time, the Israelites became convinced that Moses was either dead or missing and decided to solve what they perceived as a leadership vacuum. They convinced Aaron, the brother of Moses, to create a golden idol in the shape of a calf so they could worship it as the god who had brought them out of Egypt. God was greatly angered and told Moses that he was going to destroy every one of them and raise up a new chosen people through Moses. He pleaded with God to change his mind and spare the Israelite people.

Background Information about Moses

Moses was born to Israelite parents in Egypt during a time that they were oppressed by the Egyptians. There was a law in effect at that time that all newborn male children were to be put to death. Moses' mother hid him in a papyrus basket and set him afloat in the Nile River in order to spare his life. He was discovered and adopted by Pharaoh's daughter and raised as a prince of Egypt in the royal household of the very people who sought to destroy him. Moses still had a love for the people of his own ethnicity despite his lavish upbringing. He never forgot who he was and the humble beginnings he had come from. He eventually was forced to flee Egypt in fear of his life about the age of forty after murdering an Egyptian whom he witnessed beating a Hebrew. After leaving Egypt, Moses settled in the country of Midian where he married Jethro's daughter.

Moses then lives as a shepherd for forty years until God called him to return back to Egypt on a divine mission to set the Hebrew people free from slavery. He then returned to Egypt to become the spiritual leader of the Israelites and was used by God to perform many miraculous signs that convinced Pharaoh to free his people. Moses then led the Israelites into the Promised Land of Canaan to find a new homeland. He encountered many problems as a spiritual leader of the Israelites. They often wanted to go in one direction while he was trying to take them in a different direction spiritually. He experienced the frustration that many spiritual leaders face when trying to lead people who have not seen or do not believe in the vision provided by God.

Key Elements of Moses' Prayer

1. *Moses was praying for others and not himself.* The prayer that Moses made was similar to Elijah's prayer for Israel in that it was an intercessory prayer for others. This is what I like to refer to as the Pastor's Prayer. Moses was trying to assuage the anger of God and prevent him from destroying the emerging nation of Israel while Elijah was trying to turn the Israelites back to God. The Israelites had just been miraculously delivered from being slaves to the greatest world power at the time through many great signs and wonders.

Despite all of this, the Israelites gave their thanks and

worship to a false god for their deliverance. This happens many times when people go from being in a bad situation to a better one and feel that they no longer require the assistance of God or the ministry that helped them. They often feel the need to break free from what they believe are restrictive rules and authority. These ungrateful people then choose their own "god" or some other idol which they feel is responsible for their success. When God becomes angry about what he feels is a lack of appreciation, the spiritual leader is put into the precarious situation of having to intercede of behalf of the sinner or let God's anger burn against them. Because God's love, grace and mercy is preached so much, we sometimes forget that God gets angry from time to time at mankind's idolatrous ways. Moses could have let God destroy the Israelites (and had far fewer problems in his own life) but he chose not to. He chose to pray for those who did not feel the need to pray for themselves. By doing this, he showed that he was unselfish and in the process became one of God's greatest intercessors.

We should never forget that we are saved and blessed because of the prayers of the ministry and not just our own actions. The prayers of God's ministry aid us in being where we are today, not just our own actions. If you are saved it is likely because the love of God touched someone to preach and to pray for your soul…never forget that.

1. *Moses was and intercessor.* Webster's dictionary defines and intercessor as: *a mediator; one who interposes between parties at variance, with a view to reconcile them; one who pleads in behalf of another.* The primary purpose of Moses' prayer was to reconcile Israel back to God. He took up the cause of the Israelites and made preserving them his burden. He argued on their behalf as a spiritual attorney making a case for them to not be exterminated. God's judgment was harsh and the Israelites were in danger of being eliminated as a people. The prayer that Moses made ensured that this did not occur. He successfully reconciled the two parties even though the Israelites had nothing to say for themselves. When God becomes angry at mankind's foolish disregard for sin, he often looks for intercessors to give him a reason to show mercy:

"And he saw that there was no man, and wondered that there was no <u>intercessor</u>: therefore his arm brought salvation unto him; and his righteousness, it sustained him." Isaiah 59:16

"<u>And I sought for a man</u> among them that should make up the hedge, and stand in the gap before me for the land, <u>that I should not destroy it:</u> but I found none." Ezekiel 22:30

"I exhort therefore, that, first of all, supplications, prayers, <u>intercessions</u>, and giving of thanks, be made for

all men; for kings, and for all that are in authority; that we may lead a quiet and peaceable life in all godliness and honesty. For this is good and acceptable in the sight of God our Saviour; who will have <u>all men to be saved</u>, and to come unto the knowledge of the truth." 1 Timothy 2:1-4

God is looking for people to take up the cause of intercessory prayer. He needs people to intercede on the behalf of those who cannot or will not pray for themselves so that reconciliation can take place. The North American judicial system provides a public defender for those who have been charged with a crime and cannot defend themselves. The reason for this is so that everyone has a fair chance to be defended of the charges laid against them. As Christians we need to be sensitive to God's Holy Spirit to see if we are being beckoned as "public defenders" in the area of intercessory prayer. Who knows how many souls may be spared by our prayers?

1. *Moses gave a valid cause as to why the Israelites should be spared.* If intercessory prayer is to be effective it must be able to influence God. He wants to show mercy and compassion. The problem is often that the preponderance of the evidence of sin and idolatry is against mankind. This is why Christian intercessors must plead the blood of Jesus Christ and the power of the cross for those who are not underneath its power or have refused to submit to it. 1Timothy 2:5

tells us that Christ is the one true mediator between God and mankind. When the sins of mankind begin to weigh on God's conscience, it is our job to remind him of what Christ did on the cross and use that as a bridge between peace and destruction. Why would God need reminding of what he has already done? That's exactly what Moses did when he argued Israel's cause. He reminded the Lord that Egypt and their gods were humiliated by His awesome power and to turn around and destroy the Israelites now would let the Egyptians know that he only saved his people to kill them later. Moses also reminded God that he had made a promise to Abraham, Isaac and Jacob (called Israel) to bring them into the land of Canaan and multiply their descendants. Exodus 32:14 says that God reconsidered destroying the Israelites after listening to Moses' prayer. Does God need convincing from time to time? Absolutely.

The Result of Moses' Prayer

The Israelite people were spared God's wrath as a result of Moses' prayer. Moses successfully turned the righteous and destructive anger of an omnipotent God by reminding him of the original intentions he had for his people. A lot can be said about this. It tells us that people are able to sway the heart of God and change His mind. We may think that we have little influence in the spiritual realm but our prayers can save souls and affect the eternal destiny of the universe.

9

JACOB'S PRAYER AT PENIEL

The Prayer

"And he said, Let me go, for the day breaketh. And he said, I will not let thee go, except thou bless me." Genesis 32:26

What was Jacob praying for?

Jacob requested the angel of the Lord (actually God himself) to bless him. The request is open ended in that he does not ask for any specific thing, just to be blessed. From what we read in Genesis chapter thirty-three, we can only guess that Jacob was probably in fear of his brother Esau and asking God to protect him from their imminent meeting.

Background Information about Jacob

Jacob is the grandson of Abraham and the second of the twin sons of Isaac and Rebecca. Jacob's rivalry with his brother Esau began at childbirth when he pulled at his brother's foot. From then on, he lived up to the name he was given, which means heel catcher or sup-planter. Jacob constantly sought ways to claim his brother's inheritance, due to the tradition of the first-born male child receiving the larger portion of the inheritance at that time. He likely knew too, that there was a good chance of Esau inheriting the spiritual blessings God had promised to Abraham's descendants. The two brothers came to resent one another as they grew older and their rivalry developed into hatred. Their mother favored Jacob, while their father favored Esau. Jacob eventually tricked his brother into giving away his spiritual birthright over a pot of red beans. (Genesis 25:29-34) Later, with the aid of his mother, he put animal skins onto himself and fooled his father into giving him the natural inheritance of the firstborn.(Genesis 27)

This final incident sparked a murderous intent in Esau that forced Jacob to run away in fear of his life. He fled to his uncle Laban's house on the advice of his mother. While there, he fell in love with Laban's daughter, Rachael. Later, he found himself the victim of trickery, as he was deceived into marrying Leah, the sister of Rachael on the eve of his wedding. He found himself in trouble again as a conflict arose over grim work conditions and his scheme to steal cattle from his uncle. This caused him to flee his uncle's household and return to his homeland in Canaan. On his way home, Jacob learned that his brother Esau had become a powerful man and was on his way to seek revenge against him. It was under these circumstances that Jacob made this prayer.

When we look at Jacob's life, we can see that he had a turbulent existence due the decisions he made to deceive people. By his own admission the days of his life were "few and evil." (Genesis 47:9) God protected Jacob despite his character flaws. Jacob found himself in prayer often due to the dangerous circumstances he found himself in and received miraculous visions and blessing from God. Ten of the sons that he sired became heads of the twelve tribes of Israel, from which all Jewish people trace their heritage.

Key Elements of the Jacob's Prayer

1. *Jacob was willing to wrestle for a blessing.* Jacob managed to get himself into a bad situation and needed God's divine protection. This wasn't the first time he was in trouble but he usually managed to figure a way out of harm's way by his wits and a little help from God. This time, though, his brother was coming to seek revenge with four hundred armed men and Jacob's entire household was in danger of being killed. The only way out was to ask for divine protection. He knew that God was with him because of the miraculous things God had done for him previously. Genesis 28:12 tells us that Jacob had a dream that revealed a staircase going up into heaven where he saw the Lord at the top. God told him that he was going to be blessed with all that land that he was currently in, and that he would be protected by God everywhere he went. Jacob would have remembered this dream as his encounter with Esau loomed.

Genesis 32:1 tells us that after he left his uncle's household and traveled back to Canaan the angels of God met him. God was letting Jacob know personally that he was still under his divine protection. Despite this angelic encounter, Jacob was still in fear of his brother. He decided to send his family ahead of him hoping that his brother would feel compassion and spare their lives. While alone that night, Jacob encounters a man and they wrestle throughout the night until dawn. The man turns out to be the angel of the Lord (God in angelic form) and desires to leave. Jacob refuses to let him go until he provides him with a blessing. This is a very strange turn of events. We don't know why the angel was there, or what prompted the battle between them, but Jacob refuses to take no for an answer.

1. *Jacob had received spiritual blessings previously but now he encountered a situation where God declined to bless him.* He held on tightly and wouldn't let the angel of the Lord leave him. This was a bold move and quite dangerous. The angel of the Lord could have done any number of things to hurt Jacob. He held on because he felt that he did not have anything to lose. Jacob made up in his mind that he was going to fight for his right to be blessed. Blow for blow, he wrestled all night. He was not willing to admit defeat. He was wrestling for himself, his family and their descendants. He was wrestling for the spiritual heritage promised to Abraham, Isaac and himself. Jacob needed God to speak a prophetic blessing into his life that ensured he and his family would live through tomorrow

and beyond. His grandfather Abraham died not seeing the promise and Jacob was not going to let that happen to him. (Hebrews 11:8-13) How far are you willing to go in order to receive a spiritual blessing? Have you made your mind up to be blessed?

2. *Jacob was willing to pay a physical price for his blessing.* Most things that we achieve spiritually require a physical sacrifice. God requires us to actually *do* something in order to receive a blessing. We cannot just sit back and wait for heavenly handouts. The trials and difficult circumstances we endure are necessary in order to show God that we are willing to pay the price for spiritual advancement. Do you avoid prayer because it is too painful on your knees? Do you avoid fasting because you are not willing to go one, two or three days without food? Great blessings often require great physical and emotional efforts in order to achieve results.

The Result of Jacob's Prayer

Jacob's request for a blessing was answered. God changed his name from Jacob to Israel, which means, "He will rule as God." This new name symbolized his prevailing struggles with God and men. Jacob had many conflicts with people in his life who were close to him. It is my suspicion that he probably started the fight with the angel because of his many conflicts with people and the desperate situation that he was in. The struggles Jacob encountered in life caused many undue problems, but they also created opportunities for blessing and prosperity.

Jacob did not leave this encounter unscathed. The angel of the Lord touched Jacob's thigh and dislocated it because Jacob refused to release him. Many trials that we undergo in life will leave us scarred mentally, physically or emotionally for the rest of our lives. Jacob walked with a limp for the rest of his life because of this encounter but he received a great blessing. He was physically weakened in order to be spiritually strengthened. As Jacob limped to meet his brother later that day, he found that God had softened Esau's heart and dispelled years of resentment. This much-needed emotional blessing was in stark contrast to the wealth and riches Jacob normally sought after. This intangible blessing of goodwill from God saved his life, reconciled his long lost brother and ensured that his family would inherit God's promised spiritual blessings.

10

JEHOSHAPHAT'S PRAYER FOR DELIVERANCE

The Prayer

"And Jehoshaphat stood in the congregation of Judah and Jerusalem, in the house of the LORD, before the new court, And said, O LORD God of our fathers, <u>art not thou God in heaven</u>? And rulest not thou over all the kingdoms of the heathen? And in thine hand is there not power and might, so that none is able to withstand thee? Art not thou our God, who didst drive out the inhabitants of this land before thy people Israel, and gavest it to the seed of Abraham thy friend forever? And they dwelt therein, and have built thee a sanctuary therein for thy name, saying, If, when evil cometh upon us, as the sword, judgment, or pestilence, or famine, we stand before this house, and in thy presence, (for thy name is in this house,) and cry unto thee in our affliction, then thou will hear and help. And now, behold, the children of Ammon and Moab and mount Seir, whom thou wouldest not let Israel invade, when they came out of the land of Egypt, but they turned from them, and destroyed them not;

Behold, I say, how they reward us, to come to cast us out of thy possession, which thou hast given us to inherit. O our God, wilt thou not judge them? For we have no might against this great company that cometh against us; neither know we what to do: but our eyes are upon thee." 2 Chronicles 20:5-12

What was Jehoshaphat praying for?

Jehoshaphat was praying for God to save his country from a large coalition of Moabite, Ammonite and other enemy forces coming to invade the country of Judah.

Background Information about Jehoshaphat

Jehoshaphat was the fourth king of Judah and a direct descendant of David. The Lord was with him and he sought after God, as 2 Chronicles chapter seventeen tells us. It goes on to say that the kingdom of Judah became a strong military power and was firmly established under Jehoshaphat's control. He had great wealth and honor because the people of Judah and surrounding nations brought gifts and tribute to him. We are told in 2 Chronicles 20:10, that the fear of the Lord fell on all of the kingdoms surrounding Judah. Jehoshaphat removed the idolatrous places of worship and his heart was devoted to the ways of the Lord. No one had dared to make war against Judah out of respect for their status and military power up until the time the Moabites and Ammonites led a coalition army against them.

All of this shows us that Jehoshaphat was a great

leader who led Judah into a place of peace and prosperity. His major mistake came about when he married the daughter of Ahab, the wicked king of Israel, to form an alliance. The prophet Jehu met Jehoshaphat after he arrived home from nearly being killed in battle while fighting with King Ahab against the country of Aram. The prophet told him that the wrath of God would be on him for foolishly allying himself with Ahab. The large invasion that Jehoshaphat now faced was a direct result of the word that God spoke against him for his foolish actions.

Key Elements of Jehoshaphat's Prayer

1. *Jehoshaphat was willing to ask for help when he needed it.* He realized that the situation he faced was out of his control and decided to ask God for help. Jehoshaphat had exercised poor judgment in the past and now was wise enough to humble himself and seek the Lord's help in defending his nation against the overwhelming odds they faced. Many leaders, and ordinary people, are not willing to humble themselves and ask for God's help in hopeless situations. They try to figure out how to solve extremely difficult problems on their own. We should realize that if the problem is extremely overwhelming; seek God's help. God created the entire universe. He formed our little planet in six days and our frail, human body in one day....there is no problem too big for God!

There's nothing wrong with admitting a problem is

too big for us. People sometimes falsely believe that by asking someone else for help it means that they are somehow inadequate. This is not true. Jehoshaphat realized that his problem was spiritual and worldly. Some of life's problems are just too big for us and we need a big God to help us.

1. *Jehoshaphat realized that his problem was partly spiritual and not just worldly.* The invasion he faced was probably linked to the wrath that Jehu the prophet said would come upon him. This was a spiritual consequence of poor decision making. Jehoshaphat wisely realized that since his problem began and ended with God, he *needed God's* help to solve it.

2. *Jehoshaphat reminded God of His greatness and power.* Worshipping God and exalting him for his magnificence and power should be a key element in any prayer. We must realize that we have been created with the intent of glorifying God. (Isaiah 43:7) Therefore, he is more inclined to aid us when we fulfill our primary purpose of worshipping than when we do not worship Him. Giving God glory and honor motivates Him to show us favor.

God is not under any obligation not to intervene in the affairs of mankind. He has created the world, died on the cross and paid the penalty for our sins. Anything extra that he provides should be seen as his favor and blessings. We should rouse him into action with the proper love and adoration in our prayers. We are trying to please God, not a common man. He should be more highly esteemed than our celebrities, kings and heads of state. The proper way to approach God is from a point of humility and reverence. Jehoshaphat prayed with an awe-inspired heart that knew God as the Creator and supreme ruler of the universe. This verse from Psalms puts worshipping God in the proper perspective:

> *"Give unto the LORD the glory due unto his name; worship the LORD in the beauty of holiness." Psalms 29:2*

When we approach God in prayer he doesn't owe us anything. We owe him the glory. It is his air that we are breathing. His sunlight shines down on us through his sky as we stand on his planet. It is easy to forget all that God has done and is doing when we have pressing issues on our mind when we are praying. God is still glorious, magnificent and on the throne throughout all of our ups and downs. As we begin to praise him for his great power and glory, it is important to put him in his proper place so that miraculous things can happen to us in prayer. We will see that God is bigger than our problems when we uplift him instead of our problems. When Jehoshaphat lifted God up, he knew that God was capable of turning back any army. Worshipping and glorifying God in prayer minimizes the issues we are facing and maximizes the Lord's ability to solve it.

1. *Jehoshaphat reaffirmed his nation's right to exist and worship God.* Judah was being threatened with invasion. This

meant several things. First, the people of Judah would have lost control of the land that God gave to their forefathers. Second, if they were conquered, they would not be able to serve God the way that they wanted. In Jehoshaphat's mind, God should be offended by people who dared to take away the blessings he had given Israel. Jehoshaphat approached his prayer from the perspective that the people of Judah were children of God that the Moabites and Amorites were trying to harm. What father would not feel a sense of rage at someone trying to harm their defenseless children? Jehoshaphat knew that by praying to God as a Father and protector, his prayer would not go unanswered.

He tells the people in 2 Chronicles 20:15 that the battle was not theirs, but God's. Many trials that we encounter in life are not a personal attack on us, but have to do with our identity as people of God. The enemy directly or indirectly wants to take away the things that God has or will give us. Victory is close at hand when we realize that many of our battles don't belong to us and should not be fought by us. Our responsibility is to let the battle be fought *through* us by shifting spiritual command of the battle over to the Lord in prayer.

1. *Jehoshaphat had no doubt that God was going to answer his prayer.* He continued to pray and have faith in God even though he had previously been cursed for making foolish choices. Jehoshaphat understood that

your past mistake does not always determine your present deliverance. He understood that God is merciful and the right prayers can soften his heart. Jehoshaphat's deliverance came about as a result of understanding how to pray and what to say. Showing humility, worshipping God and including certain aspects of Israel's history roused God into acting favorably on Judah's behalf. Jehoshaphat told the people in 2 Chronicles 20:20 that when they have faith in God and his prophets, success will follow. Jehoshaphat believed their triumph and deliverance was as good as done when he finished praying. He told the people in verse twenty one to praise and worship God as their army went out to battle. Their faith was evident because they praised God for what he was going to do *before* it was done. If you really trust that God will answer your prayer, don't wait until the struggle is over…praise him in the midst of it!

The Result of Jehoshaphat's Prayer

2 Chronicles 20:22 tells us that the Lord set ambushes against the enemy to defeat them. Verse twenty three says that the enemy rose up and actually destroyed one another. When Judah arrived at the site of the battle, they did not have to fight because the enemy was *already defeated*. In addition, there was a vast amount of wealth, equipment, clothing and other valuable items left behind by the enemy…more than Judah could take away. It took three days to collect it all!

Jehoshaphat and the people of Judah went from being in fear of their lives and possibly losing everything to being victorious and gaining more financial wealth than they could carry. This was a complete reversal of fortune. We should not fear trials because God is able to do more than deliver us when we put our complete trust in him. A spiritual or financial blessing often accompanies the end of our trial as God's reward for trusting in him. Several scriptures tell us that God is able to do more than what we ask when we go through trials and pray:

"Thou preparest a table before me in the presence of mine enemies: thou anointest my head with oil; my cup runneth over." Psalms 23:5

"Now unto him that is able to do exceeding abundantly above all that we ask or think, according to the power that worketh in us." Ephesians 3:20

Jehoshaphat's prayer teaches us that we should not be dismayed when faced with overwhelming trouble. The right kind of prayer combined with faith can bring deliverance and exceeding rewards.

SUMMARY

Prayer is the greatest tool we have available to us as Christians and is useful in all situations. To Jehoshaphat, prayer became a weapon of defense and of mass destruction. For Joshua, a cosmic force arrested heavenly bodies. It became the ultimate judge and equalizer for Hannah. Prayer was a healing force for Hezekiah and a tool of mediation with Moses and Elijah. It can be whatever you need, whenever you need it.

You do not have to be an expert in order to pray. Profound vocabularies and long speeches are not necessary. From what we have examined, simpler words, and even mere thoughts, have been the tools of choice. Broken bodies, contrite spirits and humble hearts will draw God's attention and incline him to *add* more than what you asked. In summary - prayer is powerful.

There is nothing that humanity can build, create or imagine that can ever equal the efficacy of prayer. This tool was given to us by the Almighty as something anyone and everyone can use to achieve miraculous results. It has been designed that way. Whether you are standing between sins, staring imminent destruction, bankrupt or bleeding, high or low, rich or poor, PRAYER, IS FOR YOU. My hope is that after reading this book, *yours* will be the next great prayer.

God bless, and keep praying.

Pray without ceasing. 1 Thessalonians 5:17

APPENDIX : OTHER GREAT PRAYERS OF THE BIBLE

Healing Prayers

Hezekiah's Prayer for Healing (2 Kings 20)
Elijah's Prayer for the Widow's Son (1 Kings 17:20-22)
Man with Son who could not Speak or Hear (Mark 9:24)
Canaanite Woman Whose Daughter was Demon Possessed (Matthew 15:22-28)

Prayers for Deliverance

David's Prayer for God's Help (Psalm 13)
Esther and the Nation of Israel Prayer & Fasting (Esther 4 & 5)
Elisha's Prayer (2 Kings 6:15-18)
Ezra's Prayer & Fasting (Ezra 8:21-23)
Jacob's Deliverance from Esau (Genesis 32:9-12)
Jonah (Jonah 2:2-9)

Prayers for Intercession

Abraham's Intercession for Sodom & Gomorrah (Genesis 18:23-33)
Daniel's Prayer (Daniel 9:4-19)
Moses' Intercession for Miriam (Numbers 12:13)
Moses' Prayer for Israel (Deuteronomy 9:26-29)
Nehemiah's Prayer & Fasting (Nehemiah 1:3-11)
Nehemiah and Israel Prayer & Fasting (Nehemiah 9:5-38)
Jesus Prayer of Intercession (John 17:6-26)
Paul for the Ephesians (Ephesians 3:14-21)

Paul for the Colossians (Colossians 1:9-17)

Prayers for Blessing

Jabez's Prayer for Blessing (1 Chronicles 4:9-10)
Moses and the Lord (Exodus 33:12-13 Exodus 33:18)
Moses (Exodus 33:15, 16)
Solomon's Prayer for (Wisdom 1 Kings 3:6-9)
Solomon's Prayer to Dedicate the Temple (1 Kings 8:23-61)

Prayers of Thanksgiving

David's Prayer/Song of Thanks (1 Chronicles 16:7-36)
Hannah's Prayer of Thanksgiving (1 Samuel 2:1-10)
Jesus Prayer of Thanksgiving (Matthew 11:25-26)

Prayers for Strength

Samson (Judges 16:28)

Other Prayers

David's Prayer for Protection (Psalm 3)
David's Prayer for Favor (Psalm 4)
David's Prayer for Guidance (Psalm 5)
David's Prayer for Mercy (Psalm 6)
David's Prayer from Persecution (Psalm 7)
David's Prayer (Psalm 23)
David's Prayer for Trust (Psalm 25)
David's Prayer & Fasting (Psalm 35)
David's Prayer for Forgiveness (Psalm 51)
The Lord's Prayer (Matthew 6:9-13 & Luke 11:2-4)
Jesus Forgiving Those Who Crucified Him (Luke 23:34)
Apostles for Divine Direction (Acts 1:24, 25)
Apostles & Believer's Prayer to be Witnesses of the Gospel

(Acts 4:24-31)
Stephen Forgiving His Murderers (Acts 7:60)

Other Books by Benjamin Reynolds

Discover other titles at
http://amazon.com/author/benjaminreynolds

For information, contact Benjamin L. Reynolds at
info@benjaminlreynolds.com or www.benjaminlreynolds.com

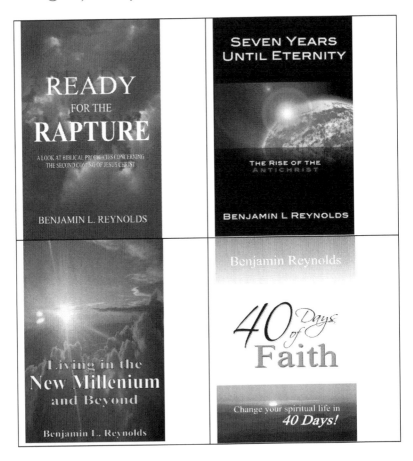

15917186R00050

Made in the USA
Lexington, KY
24 June 2012